60 Writing Topics

Practical Activities for Using Text Types

- **Procedure**
- **Narrative**
- **Explanation**
- **Report**
- **Discussion**
- **Recount**

Titles in this series:
0658 Lower Primary
0659 Middle Primary
0660 Upper Primary

Maureen Hyland

Prim-Ed
Publishing

www.prim-ed.com

0659UK

60 WRITING TOPICS *(Middle)*

First published in 2003 by R.I.C. Publications®
Reprinted under licence in 2003 by Prim-Ed Publishing

Copyright© Maureen Hyland 2003

ISBN 978-1-86400-791-6
PR–0659

Other titles available in this series:

60 WRITING TOPICS *(Lower)*
60 WRITING TOPICS *(Upper)*

Prim-Ed Publishing
Marshmeadows
New Ross
Co. Wexford

www.prim-ed.com

This master may only be reproduced by the original purchaser for use with their class(es). The publisher prohibits the loaning or onselling of this master for the purposes of reproduction.

Copyright Notice

Blackline masters or copy masters are published and sold with a limited copyright. This copyright allows publishers to provide teachers and schools with a wide range of learning activities without copyright being breached. This limited copyright allows the purchaser to make sufficient copies for use within their own education institution. The copyright is not transferable, nor can it be onsold. Following these instructions is not essential but will ensure that you, as the purchaser, have evidence of legal ownership to the copyright if inspection occurs.

For your added protection in the case of copyright inspection, please complete the form below. Retain this form, the complete original document and the invoice or receipt as proof of purchase.

Name of Purchaser:

_____

Date of Purchase:

_____

Supplier:

_____

School Order# (if applicable):

_____

Signature of Purchaser:

_____

Internet websites

In some cases, websites or specific URLs may be recommended. While these are checked and rechecked at the time of publication, the publisher has no control over any subsequent changes which may be made to webpages. It is *strongly* recommended that the class teacher checks *all* URLs before allowing pupils to access them.

View all pages online **Website:** www.prim-ed.com

Foreword

So much of life centres around the written language. This means of communication begins to influence our lives from our earliest days. It is therefore important that in educating young people we expose them to, and encourage them to become skilled in using, the many different forms of writing that will become important to them at different stages in their lives.

60 Writing Topics–Middle Primary has been designed to help teachers promote and develop many different writing skills while covering a number of different areas of the curriculum. It allows both teachers and pupils to examine units in science, technology and PSHE by encouraging pupils to use their prior knowledge of a topic, their imagination, their personal experience and personal opinion. These and many other learning skills are highlighted in the different writing tasks that the pupils are asked to complete within each of the six units.

Other titles in this series include:
60 Writing Topics Lower Primary
60 Writing Topics Upper Primary

Contents

Teachers Notes	Page ii – iv
Suggestions for Use	Page iv – v
Motivational Ideas	Page v
Curriculum Links	Page vi
Teacher Checklist	Page vii
Pupil Checklist	Page viii
Pupil Text Type Checklist	Page ix
Portfolio Proformas	Page x – xvi
Pupil Self-assessment	Page xvii
Comparison of Text Types	Page xviii
Conversion of Text Types	Page xix
Creating Writing Topics	Page xx
Merit Certificates	Page xxi

My body and how it works

What can I remember?	Recount	Page 1
How do we survive?	Report	Page 1
Let's stay active	Procedure	Page 2
From a different viewpoint	Narrative	Page 2
The process of digestion	Explanation	Page 3
What do you think?	Discussion	Page 3
Step by step	Recount	Page 4
The artist in action	Procedure	Page 4
Why is it so?	Explanation	Page 5
The creature with two legs	Narrative	Page 5

Transport

And off we go!	Report	Page 6
How does it work?	Explanation	Page 6
Do you agree?	Discussion	Page 7
Way out on the ocean	Narrative	Page 7
Thinking back	Recount	Page 8
Inside the garage	Report	Page 8
Making a paper aeroplane	Procedure	Page 9
My old go-kart	Narrative	Page 9
Designs of the past and present	Discussion	Page 10
My travel journal	Recount	Page 10

Life cycles

Quack, quack!	Report	Page 11
Caught in a web	Procedure	Page 11
A day in the life of an ant	Narrative	Page 12
Oh, what a sting!	Discussion	Page 12
From Tommy Tadpole to Thomas Frog	Report	Page 13
An amazing work of art	Explanation	Page 13
Cracked open	Procedure	Page 14
Tiny but so strong	Discussion	Page 14
Way back then	Recount	Page 15
An amazing experience	Narrative	Page 15

The sun and the planets

Day and night	Explanation	Page 16
Memories that will last forever	Recount	Page 16
Ready to blast off	Procedure	Page 17
How should the money be used?	Discussion	Page 17
An unbelievable sighting	Narrative	Page 18
An amazing event in history	Report	Page 18
The seasons	Explanation	Page 19
Oh, what a feeling	Recount	Page 19
Locating information	Procedure	Page 20
Put it in writing	Report	Page 20

Energy

Before electricity	Procedure	Page 21
The windmill	Explanation	Page 21
Through the eyes of a spider	Narrative	Page 22
Experimenting with magnets	Procedure	Page 22
When I was young	Recount	Page 23
Do we use too much electricity?	Discussion	Page 23
We need the sun	Explanation	Page 24
Fossil fuels	Report	Page 24
The ride of my life	Narrative	Page 25
Safety first	Report	Page 25

Leisure time

Is there time to be bored?	Discussion	Page 26
The greatest day	Recount	Page 26
My favourite toy	Explanation	Page 27
A new board game	Procedure	Page 27
Inside and outside	Discussion	Page 28
A star for one show	Narrative	Page 28
So much time for fun	Recount	Page 29
How a jack-in-the-box works	Explanation	Page 29
Warnings are important	Discussion	Page 30
How do we spend our time?	Report	Page 30

Teachers Notes

There are ten writing cards for each unit: each card asks the pupil to use a different writing skill. While the teacher will be able to assess the pupil's understanding of the content of a specific unit of study, these writing cards will, most importantly, allow the teacher to evaluate the pupil's understanding of, and ability to use, many different forms of writing. Tasks involve using skills in narrative, recount, report, procedure, discussion and explanatory writing. Because of the nature of the tasks, pupils can complete them individually, thus allowing all pupils in a class to attempt a large variety of activities.

Each page contains two writing tasks on a particular topic. An icon indicates the unit of work each task belongs to. The icons below show the relevant units for which the cards have been written:

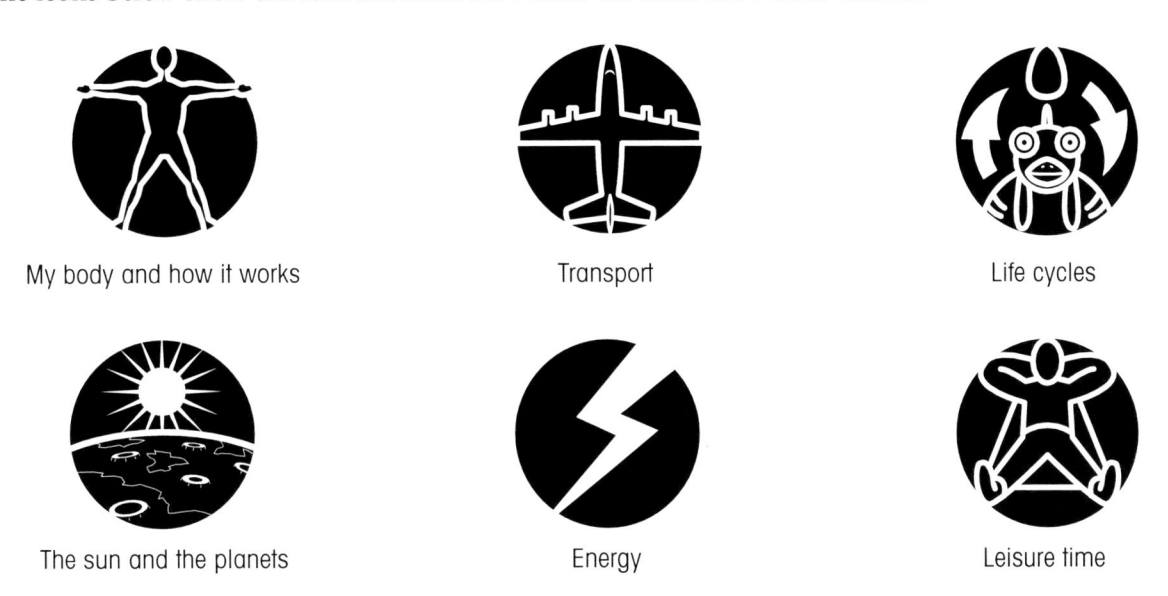

My body and how it works

Transport

Life cycles

The sun and the planets

Energy

Leisure time

The writing cards can be copied onto coloured or plain card and laminated for protection. They can be placed in a central location for pupils to access easily. The tasks can be assigned by the teacher or the pupils may choose their own.

A pupil checklist has been provided for the pupils to record the cards used. A teacher checklist has also been included so the teacher can monitor the progress of the class and ensure that all pupils are practising each writing genre. This may be enlarged to display in the room. Pupils should choose cards which cover a variety of writing genres. Should a teacher wish to assign a writing task as a class or group activity, multiple copies may be made. Teachers may find these invaluable during literacy lessons.

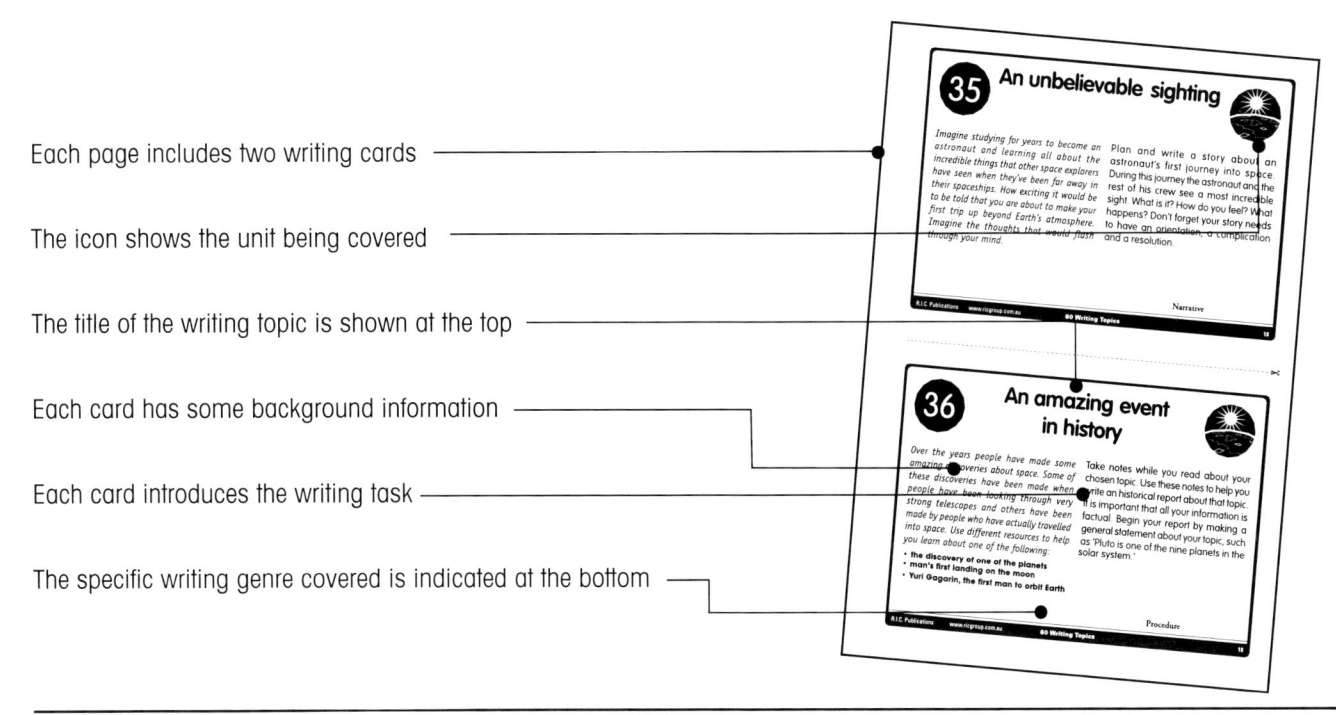

- Each page includes two writing cards
- The icon shows the unit being covered
- The title of the writing topic is shown at the top
- Each card has some background information
- Each card introduces the writing task
- The specific writing genre covered is indicated at the bottom

Teachers Notes

What to Look for When Assessing a Pupil's Understanding of a Particular Genre

The following information provides the teacher with a definition of each of the writing genres, an outline of the structure of the texts and some of the specific language features, that when used, show an understanding of the genre in question. Not all of the language features will be evident in the texts of middle primary pupils, but this outline will enable the teacher to monitor the progress of the pupils as their writing skills develop.

Narrative

Definition of a narrative: A narrative is a text that tells a story, often in chronological sequence. Narratives are generally imaginative but can be based on factual information. Narratives can take on a variety of forms such as short stories, myths, poems and fairytales.

Text structure: A narrative consists of three parts:

(a) an orientation or introduction, where the setting is presented, characters introduced and time set for the event/s to occur.
(b) a complication, where problems arise concerning the main character(s).
(c) a resolution where the problems of the character/s are resolved.

Special language features: use of words that link stages in time, descriptive enhancement by use of adjectives and adverbs, use of action verbs to highlight physical and mental processes and can be written in first or third person.

Recount

Definition of a recount: A recount is a text that tells about past experiences or events, written for information or entertainment. They can be based on the author's personal experience, on historical events or it can be imaginative, whereby the author has no direct link to recalled events.

Text structure: Most recounts begin with some form of orientation where the who? what? when? where? and why? of the text are introduced. This is followed by a chronologically ordered set of events. There can be some form of concluding statement or reorientation at the end.

Special language features: use of past tense, correct sequencing of events, words related to time, inclusion of action verbs and personal comments.

Report

Definition of a report: A report is a text that consists of an organised factual record of events or a classification and description of one or many things. It can be related to the present day or be based around something from the past.

Text structure: Begins with a general statement or introduction that indicates the nature of the topic upon which the report is based. This is followed by a description of the various features relevant to the topic. In some cases this can take on the form of 'named' paragraphs or subheadings. It can conclude with a summarising statement.

Special language features: vocabulary related to specific topic, action verbs, words identifying classifications and descriptive language.

Procedure

Definition of a procedure: A procedure explains how to make or do something.

Text structure: Most procedural texts begin with an outline of what is to be achieved, or an aim. This is followed by a list of required materials and then step by step instructions to reach the goal. The text can conclude with an evaluation.

Special language features: words of commands, time-related connectives, sequential ordering of steps, action verbs, and detailed information, for example, size, amount, weight.

Discussion

Definition of a discussion: A discussion text aims to present and develop ideas in the form of a logical argument. The text can be one sided, or, it can address both sides of an argument allowing the reader to form an opinion from the information presented.

Text structure: Most discussions begin with a statement which introduces the issue that will be addressed. This is followed by arguments with evidence to support the stance. A conclusion summarises the presentation or suggests that the reader now form an opinion.

Special language features: use of topic-related vocabulary, use of connectives to reinforce results of actions, thinking verbs used to express opinion and the use of emotive and persuasive language.

Explanation

Definition of an explanation: An explanation is a text that outlines how or why things occur, or how things operate.

Text structure: An explanatory text begins with a statement about what is to be explained. This is followed by details of sequential events or stages in operation. It usually ends with some form of concluding statement.

Special language features: use of topic-specific vocabulary, words that outline cause and effect and words identifying time relationships, for example, following, then; and the use of present tense.

Suggestions for Use

The writing tasks included in this book are intended to be a multi-use resource for the teacher in the classroom. Therefore, the suggestions listed below are in no way definitive, but just some of the possible uses. Teachers should choose only those activities which are appropriate to the ability levels and literacy experiences of their pupils.

Specific writing genre tasks

Each writing genre is explained carefully on pages iii–iv, showing a definition of the genre, the structure and special language features of the text. After pupils have been exposed to each specific genre, the writing topics may be used to reinforce their concept of the genre.

An assessment text type checklist has been included on page ix. The features of each text type have been included with tick boxes for the teacher to monitor and record pupils' use of the structures and features of each genre. Some features will be too difficult for middle primary pupils, so these assessment records should be passed to the next teacher. As pupils become more able, it may be appropriate to provide them with their own copy of page ix, to enable them to assess their own progress.

Writing specific to a particular theme

Each of the six themes has ten writing topics relating to it. Teachers who are covering a particular theme will be able to utilise the writing topics to reinforce and add interest to the theme.

Portfolio assessment tasks

The writing tasks may be used as a literacy assessment activity, after the pupils have been exposed to and practised the specific writing genres. To assist teachers to use the writing topics in this way, a portfolio proforma has been included. The pupil's writing topic activity may be stapled to the proforma. A checklist assists the teacher to assess whether the pupil has included the structures and features necessary for that particular genre. Other aspects of literacy, such as spelling and grammar, may be assessed at the same time. A sample proforma for each text type is included on pages xi to xvi. A blank proforma may be found on page x.

Class/Group/Individual literacy activities

The writing topics may be used during class or group literacy lessons, with specific topics or tasks given to individuals or groups. Alternatively, the whole class could be working on the same writing task. Multiple copies of a particular card may be made for class or group work.

Pupil self-assessment

Pupil self-assessment, using the pupil checklist, allows the pupils to monitor their progress in the use of specific writing genres. As pupils become more familiar with the features and structures of each writing genre, they will be able to monitor their increased use of these in each writing genre. This self-assessment format may be useful for the pupil to use when involved in three-way conferences among parents, the teacher and himself/herself. A sample proforma is included on page xvii.

Comparison/Conversion of text types

Using the writing topics, the teacher may compare one writing genre with another. Pupils can observe and use the different structures and features within their own writing. Pupils may be required to convert one text type into another, making sure to include the relevant structures and features. A format for comparing text types is included on page xviii. A proforma to convert one text type to another is included on page xix.

Extension/Reinforcement activities

Every classroom has pupils of varying abilities, talents, working habits and personalities. Pupils who are fast workers may be rewarded with their choice of a writing topic to complete until the other pupils finish. Pupils who have difficulty completing a specific writing genre may be given writing topics to reinforce that particular genre, as long as they have not completed the task before.

*Creating writing topics

Using the writing topics as a guide, the pupils may be required to create writing topics of their own relating to a specific writing genre. These topics may be exchanged within the class, completed and evaluated. A writing topic which many pupils have difficulty completing may not be suitable for the specific writing genre. A writing topic which pupils can easily shape to suit a specific genre is a suitable writing topic. A blank proforma to enable pupils to create their own writing topics is included on page xx.

*This type of activity is only suitable for very competent or older pupils.

Reinforcement/Assessment of features of language/handwriting

Using the writing topic, the teacher may be able to evaluate the pupil's knowledge of grammar concepts, punctuation, spelling and handwriting. One task may be used to assess or reinforce a number of objectives. This can be a timesaver activity for the teacher.

Planning/Reviewing/Changing text types

The planning of a writing form can be complex and daunting for pupils. An obvious format, with specific structures and features, allows the pupils the security to write personal topics within a given framework, while still allowing some flexibility.

Modelling Writing

Teachers may use similar titles for particular themes to model the different writing genre for the pupils. Try to avoid using those exact titles used in the writing topics so that pupils are creating their own ideas when using the task cards.

Motivational Ideas

Pupils need motivation to encourage creative ideas. Since the writing topics are being used as an individual activity, it is difficult to inspire each pupil before he or she begins each writing topic. The following ideas are suggested as a reference for pupils to use before they begin their writing topic:

- Teachers could provide visual displays of particular themes near the writing topics box; for example, toys brought in by the pupils, photographs, newspaper clippings and posters. When displays are changed, each display can be recorded on camera and photographs and digital pictures displayed for other pupils to view.
- Pupils who finish quickly may find extra pictures in magazines to add to class books on particular themes.
- Banks of word lists for particular themes can be recorded and displayed for future reference.
- Displays of other pupils' work on the same topic may be viewed to encourage ideas.
- Display theme books from the library relevant to a particular writing theme.
- Provide and display outlines of the writing forms for pupils to refer to when writing (see page iii–iv).
- Where possible, allow pupils access to a computer to research a particular theme or writing topic.

Curriculum Links

The activities in this book are designed to encourage pupils to demonstrate the following objectives.

60 Writing Topics Book	Country	Year/Level	Subject/Strand	Objective
Middle	England	3	Literacy, Term 1, Text Level Work	• (11) develop the use of settings in stories • (15) begin to organise stories into paragraphs • (21) make a simple record of information from texts read • (22) write simple non-chronological reports
			Literacy, Term 2, Text Level Work	• (9) write story plan for own myth • (16) write instructions using a range of organisational devices
			Literacy, Term 3, Text Level Work	• (12) write a first person account • (16) write letters
		4	Literacy, Term 1, Text Level Work	• (15) use paragraphs in story writing • (24) write newspaper style reports • (25) write clear instructions • (27) write a non-chronological report
			Literacy, Term 2, Text Level Work	• (23) collect information from a variety of sources and present it in one format • (25) write explanations of a process
			Literacy, Term 3, Text Level Work	• (23) present a point of view in writing
	Northern Ireland	KS2	English, Writing	• plan written work, when appropriate • write for a variety of purposes, including to: inform; explain; describe; narrate; report; persuade; express a point of view and give instructions • know for whom they are writing and be aware of the needs of the particular audience • write in a variety of forms and develop control of their different conventions, including: stories; creative and imaginative writing; diaries; poems; letters; descriptions; reports and instructions • present and structure ideas, information and opinions
	Scotland	B/C	English Language, Writing	• write in an appropriate form and with adequate vocabulary to communicate key events, facts or ideas • write about a personal experience for a specific purpose and audience, using appropriate organisation and vocabulary • write an imaginative story or poem, using appropriate organisation and vocabulary
	Wales	KS2	English, Writing	• (1.3) write in response to a wide range of stimuli • (1.4) use the characteristics of different kinds of writing • (1.5) write in forms which include imaginative and non-fiction writing • (2.1) use writing as a means of developing, organising and communicating ideas • (2.4) develop their ability to organise and structure their writing in a variety of ways

Teacher Checklist

Use this chart to record the WRITING TOPICS that have been completed

Pupil Name	My body and how it works	Transport	Life cycles	The sun and the planets	Energy	Leisure time
	1 2 3 4 5 6 7 8 9 10	11 12 13 14 15 16 17 18 19 20	21 22 23 24 25 26 27 28 29 30	31 32 33 34 35 36 37 38 39 40	41 42 43 44 45 46 47 48 49 50	51 52 53 54 55 56 57 58 59 60

Pupil Checklist

Use this chart to record the WRITING TOPICS that have been completed

My Body and how it works

1	2	3	4	5	6	7	8	9	10
How can I remember?	How do we survive?	Let's stay active	From a different viewpoint	The process of digestion	What do you think?	Step by step	The artist in action	Why is it so?	The creature with two legs

Comment _____

The sun and the planets

31	32	33	34	35	36	37	38	39	40
Day and night	Memories that will last forever	Ready to blast off	How should the money be used?	An unbelievable sighting	An amazing event in history	The seasons	Oh, what a feeling	Locating information	Put it in writing

Comment _____

Transport

11	12	13	14	15	16	17	18	19	20
And off we go!	Do you agree?	Way out on the ocean	Thinking back	Inside the garage	Making a paper aeroplane	My old go-kart	Designs of the past and present	My travel journal	

Comment _____

Energy

41	42	43	44	45	46	47	48	49	50
Before electricity	The windmill	Through the eyes of a spider	Experimenting with magnets	When I was young	Do we use too much electricity?	We need the sun	Fossil fuels	The ride of my life	Safety first

Comment _____

Life cycles

21	22	23	24	25	26	27	28	29	30
Quack, quack	Caught in a web	A day in the life of an ant	Oh, what a sting!	From Tommy Tadpole to Thomas Frog	An amazing work of art	Cracked open	Tiny but so strong	Way back then	An amazing experience

Comment _____

Leisure Time

51	52	53	54	55	56	57	58	59	60
Is there time to be bored?	The greatest day	My favourite toy	A new board game	Inside and outside	A star for one show	So much time for fun	How a jack-in-the-box works	Warnings are important	How do we spend our time?

Comment _____

Prim-Ed Publishing – www.prim-ed.com   **60 Writing Topics**

Pupil Text Type Checklist

Name _____ Date _____

Narrative

1. Introduces the setting, time and character(s). ☐
2. Includes a sequence of events involving the main character(s). ☐
3. Includes a complication involving the main character(s). ☐
4. Includes a resolution to the complication. ☐
5. Uses a range of conjunctions to connect ideas. ☐
6. Writes in meaningful paragraphs. ☐
7. Uses descriptive language. ☐
8. Writes in the past tense. ☐

Comment _____
_____
_____
_____

Recount

1. Introduces all relevant background detail (who, when, where, why). ☐
2. Includes significant events in detail. ☐
3. Includes significant events in chronological order. ☐
4. Uses vocabulary to suggest time passing. ☐
5. Writes in paragraphs to show separate sections. ☐
6. Maintains the past tense. ☐
7. Writes a conclusion with an evaluative comment. ☐

Comment _____
_____
_____
_____

Report

1. Begins with a general or classifying statement. ☐
2. Includes accurate detailed descriptions. ☐
3. Uses factual language rather than imaginative. ☐
4. Writes in the third person. ☐
5. Writes in the present tense. ☐
6. Uses linking and action verbs. ☐

Comment _____
_____
_____
_____

Procedure

1. States the purpose of the procedure clearly and precisely. ☐
2. Lists the materials or requirements under appropriate headings or layout. ☐
3. Presents the method in a detailed, logical sequence. ☐
4. Begins instructions with an imperative verb. ☐
5. Uses subject-specific vocabulary. ☐
6. Writes in simple present tense. ☐
7. Includes an evaluation (if appropriate). ☐

Comment _____
_____
_____
_____

Discussion

1. Begins with an opening statement presenting a general view of the topic. ☐
2. Presents 'for' and 'against' arguments in a logical manner. ☐
3. Uses supporting details in presenting each argument. ☐
4. Uses an impersonal style of writing. ☐
5. Uses a variety of controlling words and conjunctions. ☐
6. Uses paragraphs to state and elaborate on each point. ☐
7. Writes an evaluative conclusion. ☐

Comment _____
_____
_____
_____

Explanation

1. Begins with a precise statement or definition. ☐
2. Includes subject-specific terms and technical vocabulary where appropriate. ☐
3. Gives a clear account in logical sequence of how and why the phenomenon occurs. ☐
4. Uses simple present tense. ☐
5. Uses linking words to show cause and effect. ☐
6. Includes an evaluation (if necessary). ☐

Comment _____
_____
_____
_____

Portfolio Proforma

Name _____ Date _____

Glue pupil writing task here.
(Staple pupil writing to the back.)

TASK The pupil was asked to write a _____ including all structures and features of the text type.

English	Writing

Objectives   Demonstrated   Needs Further Opportunity

- Writes a _____.
- Includes all structures and features.

☐ ☐
☐ ☐

Teacher Comment _____

_____

_____

_____

Portfolio Proforma – Narrative

Name _____ Date _____

Glue pupil writing task here.
(Staple pupil writing to the back.)

TASK The pupil was asked to write a narrative including all structures and features of the text type.

Objectives   Demonstrated   Needs Further Opportunity

- Writes a narrative. ☐ ☐
- Includes all structures and features.
    1. Introduces the setting, time and character(s). ☐ ☐
    2. Includes a sequence of events involving the main character(s). ☐ ☐
    3. Includes a complication involving the main character(s). ☐ ☐
    4. Includes a resolution to the complication. ☐ ☐
    5. Uses a range of conjunctions to connect ideas. ☐ ☐
    6. Writes in meaningful paragraphs. ☐ ☐
    7. Uses descriptive language. ☐ ☐
    8. Writes in the past tense. ☐ ☐

Teacher Comment _____

_____

_____

Portfolio Proforma – Recount

Name _____ Date _____

Glue pupil writing task here.
(Staple pupil writing to the back.)

TASK The pupil was asked to write a recount including all structures and features of the text type.

Objectives   Demonstrated   Needs Further Opportunity

- Writes a recount.   ☐   ☐
- Includes all structures and features.
  1. Introduces all relevant background detail (who, when, where, why).   ☐   ☐
  2. Includes significant events in detail.   ☐   ☐
  3. Includes significant events in chronological order.   ☐   ☐
  4. Uses vocabulary to suggest time passing.   ☐   ☐
  5. Writes in paragraphs to show separate sections.   ☐   ☐
  6. Maintains the past tense.   ☐   ☐
  7. Writes a conclusion with an evaluative comment.   ☐   ☐

Teacher Comment _____

_____

_____

Portfolio Proforma – Report

Name _____ Date _____

Glue pupil writing task here.
(Staple pupil writing to the back.)

TASK The pupil was asked to write a report including all structures and features of the text type.

Objectives   Demonstrated   Needs Further Opportunity

- Writes a report. ☐ ☐
- Includes all structures and features.
    1. Begins with a general or classifying statement. ☐ ☐
    2. Includes accurate detailed descriptions. ☐ ☐
    3. Uses factual language rather than imaginative. ☐ ☐
    4. Writes in the third person. ☐ ☐
    5. Writes in the present tense. ☐ ☐
    6. Uses linking and action verbs. ☐ ☐

Teacher Comment _____
_____
_____

Portfolio Proforma – Procedure

Name _____ Date _____

Glue pupil writing task here.
(Staple pupil writing to the back.)

TASK The pupil was asked to write a procedure including all structures and features of the text type.

Objectives	Demonstrated	Needs Further Opportunity
• Writes a procedure.	☐	☐
• Includes all structures and features.		
1. States the purpose of the procedure clearly and precisely.	☐	☐
2. Lists the materials or requirements under appropriate headings or layout.	☐	☐
3. Presents the method in a detailed, logical sequence.	☐	☐
4. Begins instructions with an imperative verb.	☐	☐
5. Uses subject-specific vocabulary.	☐	☐
6. Writes in a simple present tense.	☐	☐
7. Includes an evaluation (if appropriate).	☐	☐

Teacher Comment _____

_____

_____

Portfolio Proforma – Discussion

Name _____ Date _____

Glue pupil writing task here.
(Staple pupil writing to the back.)

TASK — The pupil was asked to write a discussion including all structures and features of the text type.

Objectives	Demonstrated	Needs Further Opportunity
• Writes an discussion.	☐	☐
• Includes all structures and features.		
1. Begins with an opening statement presenting a general view of the subject.	☐	☐
2. Presents 'for' and 'against' arguments in a logical manner.	☐	☐
3. Uses supporting details in presenting each argument.	☐	☐
4. Uses an impersonal style of writing.	☐	☐
5. Uses a variety of controlling words and conjunctions.	☐	☐
6. Uses paragraphs to state and elaborate on each point.	☐	☐
7. Writes an evaluative conclusion.	☐	☐

Teacher Comment _____

_____

_____

Portfolio Proforma – Explanation

Name _____ Date _____

Glue pupil writing task here.
(Staple pupil writing to the back.)

(TASK) The pupil was asked to write an explanation including all structures and features of the text type.

Objectives	Demonstrated	Needs Further Opportunity
• Writes an explanation.	☐	☐
• Includes all structures and features.		
1. Begins with a precise statement or definition.	☐	☐
2. Includes subject-specific terms and technical vocabulary.	☐	☐
3. Gives a clear account in logical sequence of how and why the phenomenon occurs.	☐	☐
4. Uses simple present tense.	☐	☐
5. Uses linking words to show cause and effect.	☐	☐
6. Includes an evaluation (if necessary).	☐	☐

Teacher Comment _____
_____
_____

Pupil Self-assessment

Name _____ Date _____

Glue pupil writing task here.
(Staple pupil writing to the back.)

Text Type _____

Features of text	Pupil Self-assessment	Features of text	Pupil Self-assessment
• _____	☺	• _____	☺
• _____	☺	• _____	☺
• _____	☺	• _____	☺
• _____	☺	• _____	☺

In my next _____, I will need to _____

_____

_____

Comparison of Text Types

Name _____ Date _____

Text Type 1 _____

Text Type 2 _____

Similar Features
_____
_____
_____
_____
_____

Different Features
_____
_____
_____
_____
_____

- Which text type has the most features? _____

- Which text type has the least features? _____

- Which text type is easier to write? Why? _____
_____

- Which is harder to write? _____

Conversion of Text Types

Name _____ Date _____

Glue pupil writing task here.
(Staple pupil writing to the back.)

In the space below, rewrite your writing topic using a different text type. Try to include all the features of the new text type.

I have chosen to convert my writing task to a _____.

_____

_____

_____

_____

_____

_____

Creating Writing Topics

Name _____ Date _____

Use the same format below to create your own writing topic.

Don't forget to include:

- a title for your writing topic
- a theme (you may draw the icon to match)
- a number for your topic
- an introduction to the topic
- the writing task
- the text type required

Ask a friend to complete your writing task.
Evaluate your writing task.
Was your friend able to use the information that you gave them to write the correct text type?

Yes/No. If not, why not? _____

_____

What changes would you make to a new writing topic? _____

Writing Wiz

Name_____ Date_____
Signed_____

Wicked Writing

Name_____ Date_____
Signed_____

Wrapped in Writing

Name_____ Date_____
Signed_____

Writing Honours awarded to

_____

Signed_____ Date_____

1 What can I remember?

When we were born we were very tiny. Most babies only weigh about three and a half kilograms and are not much more than 50 centimetres in length. Look at yourself now. You are much heavier and a lot taller than you were as a baby and even as a toddler. We don't remember when we were babies but some people can remember events that happened really early in their lives. Our brains are very active as soon as we are born and it is because of the way our brain works that we are able to remember things from the past.

Try to recall an event that took place very early in your life. It might be a birthday, a visit to somewhere special or the arrival of a baby brother or sister. Write a recount about this event, including where it took place, your age then and who or what else was involved in your experience.

Recount

---

2 How do we survive?

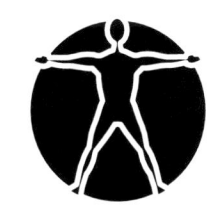

There are many organs within our bodies which have special jobs to do. Doctors do amazing operations now to help sick people get better. They are even able to transplant such things as the heart and the lungs to help sick people live longer than they otherwise would. We cannot live without such important parts in our bodies and they need to work well if we are going to remain healthy.

Choose one special part of the body such as the brain, the lungs, the liver or the stomach and find out as much information as you can about the important part it plays in the body. You could find out such facts as where this organ is situated inside the body, how it works and why it is so important. Once you have taken some brief notes in your own words, write a report about your chosen body part.

Report

3 — Let's stay active

If you are going to remain fit and healthy you need to get regular exercise. Some simple daily exercises will help to keep your muscles in good shape and your heart pumping very well. You don't have to do anything too strenuous.

Imagine that you have been given the job of running a simple exercise session for some children of your age. Before you begin you need to give the instructor at the gymnasium a copy of the exercises you plan to do. Write out step-by-step instructions for two exercises that you would try to encourage the children to undertake each day.

Procedure

---

4 — From a different viewpoint

Sometimes we wonder what sort of view birds have from high above. We can also try to imagine what the world looks like from somewhere down low, where snails slide along, in danger of being trodden on. It's time for you to stretch your imagination to the fullest. You are about to change your height!

Imagine that you have either grown to an incredible height of at least five metres or you have shrunk to about 10 centimetres. How different your world looks now! You see everything differently from those around you.

Write a story about an amazing experience you have while you are at this strange height. Remember to use descriptive language to make your story more exciting for people who are going to read it.

Narrative

5 The process of digestion

We know that it is very important for us to eat in order to remain fit and healthy. Each day we eat many different types of food and these foods are used by all different parts of the body. Once we decide we are going to eat something we pop it in our mouths and there the process of digestion begins.

Do some research about how we digest food. Take some basic notes that will help you remember what happens once you put food in your mouth. In your own words, write an explanation of how the process of digestion works. You could draw and label a simple diagram to reinforce your written information.

Explanation

---

6 What do you think?

We can learn a great deal about life from our parents. They are usually the first people who influence us and the first to teach us what is good for us. Read and think about the following statement.

Children should always eat what their parents tell them to eat.

Decide whether or not you agree with this statement. Write as many points as you can to show why you think this is right or wrong. Remember, when you are making your decision, the word 'always' is very important.

Discussion

7 Step by step

It's not very often that we stop and think how much work our feet do in one day. They get us from one place to the next from the minute we get out of bed in the morning. They take us over all types of ground at many different speeds. Do they ever get the chance to complain?

Your imagination is about to run wild. You have actually become your feet! You are at the end of an exhausting day and the only thing left for you to do before you go to bed is to write in your diary. Remember, you are your feet. Write a recount of all that you have gone through during the day.

Recount

8 The artist in action

Magazines are often full of pictures of famous people, models or people who are trying to sell us things. You are about to use these people to create your own masterpiece—a portrait of a 'new' person. But, before you begin your artistic creation, you need to write detailed instructions on how you are going to go about your task. For example, are you going to use parts from many pictures and paste them together, or cut out 'half a person' who will need to be finished with pencil?

When you have made your decision, begin by listing everything that you will need to complete the task. Follow this with clear instructions on how to go about creating the portrait.

Procedure

9 Why is it so?

Use books, the computer and any other resources available to help you research the heart. Take brief notes on the most important facts that you discover.

Use your notes and the knowledge you have about your own body to help you carry out the following task.

Write an explanation as to why your heart beats faster when you exercise. Begin by making a statement about the heart and then follow this with a description of the heart, how and why it works the way it does and the effect this has on a person. Remember to emphasise why the heart's rate of pumping changes when a person is exercising.

Explanation

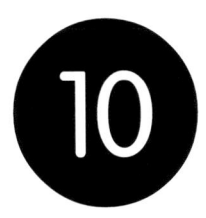

10 The creature with two legs

A myth is a story or imaginative narrative that is used to tell us about how some unusual thing occurred; for example, how the zebra got its stripes or how the kangaroo got its large tail. Often these types of stories are passed down from one generation to the next. When we look at the whole world of animals, humans have some similarities to other creatures but in other ways they are quite different.

Write a myth about why humans only walk around on two legs. Remember a narrative begins with an introduction. This is followed by the situations that lead to or create the problem and then, of course, at the end you have the resolution. Each of these sections must be included in your myth.

Narrative

11 — And off we go!

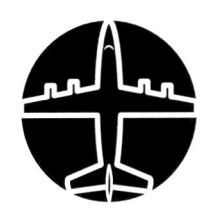

Many different forms of transport are used in sporting events and races around the world. Cars, bicycles and boats are often driven or ridden in exciting challenges. Use a number of different resources to help you find out about one special race such as the America's Cup, the Tour de France or a Formula 1 Grand Prix.

When reading information about your chosen event, take notes about the most important facts. Use these facts to help you write a report about this event. Begin your report by making a statement about the type of event it is and then describe its main features.

Report

12 — How does it work?

Once we learn how to ride a bicycle it is something we can do over and over again without really thinking about it. We climb on, decide where we want to go and we pedal away. But what makes that bicycle work?

Find a picture of a bicycle in a book or sketch one yourself. Think about what you do when you want a bicycle to move and how it actually gets into motion. In your own words, explain how this simple means of transport works.

Explanation

13 Do you agree?

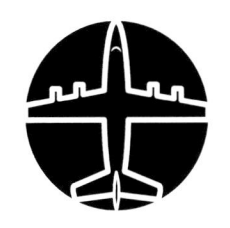

On the radio and television and in newspapers and magazines there are often statements made about traffic, the roads and the environment.

Spend a little time thinking about the following statement:

Too many people drive cars to work.

Some people will agree with this sentence and others will disagree.

What do you think?

Once you have decided whether or not you agree with the statement, write as many arguments as possible to show why you think the way you do. Begin with a statement about the issue.

Discussion

---

14 Way out on the ocean

Some people love to go on a cruise for their holidays. They sail around in very large ships, stopping off at different ports along the way. Some of these ships are so big that they seem like small cities on water. It's time for you to use your imagination.

Pretend you are sailing with your family on one of these big cruise ships. You are having great fun doing everything together until one afternoon when you get lost. After going into your family cabin to get your camera and coming back out on to the deck, you can't find anyone you know. Write about your lonely adventures.

Narrative

15 Thinking back

Perhaps you have been lucky enough to go somewhere special on an aeroplane. Even if you haven't been on an aeroplane you can imagine that you have—think about where you might have been travelling, who was with you, how you filled in your time on the journey and how you felt about the experience.

You have just arrived at your holiday destination and the first thing that you want to do is write a letter to your best friend at home telling him or her all about your trip on the aeroplane. When you write your letter, remember to put the address of where you are staying in the top right-hand corner of the page. (Don't forget, you can make this up!)

Recount

---

16 Inside the garage

Before you can write a report you need to have collected or gathered information. You are going to collect information from children in your class about different vehicles their families have at home. Once you have studied all the information they give you, you are going to write a report about the different vehicles kept for private use.

You need to rule up a chart so you can ask the children about the vehicles they have at home. You will need spaces to record their answers. You will probably want to ask if they have cars, bicycles, motorbikes, caravans, scooters or go-karts. Ask how many they have of each. Once you have looked carefully at your answers, write a report about the most common vehicles kept at the childrens' homes. Also mention other forms of transport and whether or not they are common at these homes.

Report

17 Making a paper aeroplane

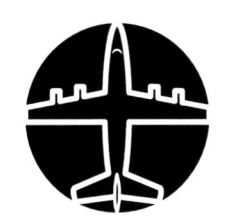

There are many things that can be made from paper. Origami is the art of folding paper to create various shapes and objects. This art was invented by people in Japan. For many years children have enjoyed making paper aeroplanes and seeing how far they can fly them. It's your turn to tell us how to do it.

You are going to write step-by-step instructions to explain how to make a paper aeroplane. You might like to try making a few before you get to the writing stage. Once you know exactly how to do it, list the materials needed and then write numbered steps that can be followed to produce an aeroplane.

Procedure

---

18 My old go-kart

Stories can be told in the form of poems. As long as we have an introduction, a complication and a resolution, we can call the poem a narrative.

The following verse is an introduction for a narrative. The story in this poem is about a go-kart. Read the following verse:

You need to finish this poem. Write about what happened and about how you ended up. It is a rhyming poem so try to keep the rhyming pattern going throughout the rest of the poem. Write four lines for each verse.

**I was rolling along in my go-kart
Dreaming of a racing car track
When suddenly I turned too sharply
And everything in front turned black.**

Narrative

19 Designs of the past and present

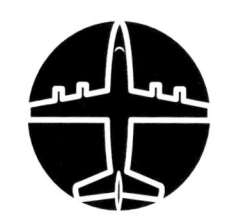

The first petrol-powered car was invented back in 1893. This car didn't look very much like those we know today but it took people from the four-legged power of a horse to the four-wheeled power of a car. I wonder how long the inventor was working on his plan for this vehicle.

Read the following statement:

People who invented cars back in the 1890s must have been more talented than people who design cars today.

This is a statement that some people will agree with while some will think it is incorrect. You need to write as many points as you can to show why this statement could be correct and then as many as you can to show why it might be incorrect. People who read your work can then make up their own minds. Begin your text by writing a general statement about car inventors and designers.

Discussion

---

20 My travel journal

To help remember the events of a holiday, some people choose to keep a travel journal. At the end of each day they write a brief summary of what they have done so they can recall things at a later date, or so they can tell friends about their adventures.

Pretend you have been on a camping holiday down by the beach. Write a brief summary of what you did each day for one week. At the top of each entry, write the day of the week.

Recount

21 Quack, quack!

We sometimes hear stories about a mother duck trying to cross a road with her newborn ducklings. Usually, that mother duck does an amazing job, reaching her destination without too much difficulty. Mother ducks are very protective of their babies. After all, they sit around for 28 days waiting for the little creatures to hatch out of their eggs.

Use a variety of resources to research the life of a duck from egg to adult. Use your information to write a report about the life cycle of a duck. You can use diagrams to reinforce your information.

Report

---

22 Caught in a web

There is nothing more fascinating than the sight of a sparkling spider web hanging on a tree on a dewy autumn morning. No matter how clever we think we are, none of us is able to do what a spider can do. But let's not be disheartened. Let's see how clever you can be.

Get yourself into an artistic frame of mind. You are going to make a spider web using simple materials such as cardboard, wool, cotton, glue and glitter. This list of materials is just an example and you might have other ideas of your own. Plan your web and then have a go at making it. Once you think you are successful you need to write clear instructions so that a friend can make an identical web. Begin by listing the materials that are needed and then number and order your instructions.

Procedure

23 — A day in the life of an ant

Have you ever stopped and watched a trail of ants and wondered how far these little creatures walk in a day, what they are up to and where they go at the end of the day? They really are amazing little creatures that always seem so busy going to and from somewhere, avoiding obstacles and sticking very close to some friends.

Write an imaginary story about the day in the life of an ant. Don't forget that all narratives need an introduction, complication and resolution. Try to make your story very descriptive by making use of adjectives and adverbs.

Narrative

---

24 — Oh, what a sting!

If you've ever been stung by a bee you'll know that it can be a very painful experience. If you haven't, try to avoid the situation. This tiny creature, though able to put us through a great deal of pain, is also able to produce delicious food we call honey. The idea of a golden-brown slice of toast spread with fresh honey is a mouth-watering thought.

While both these ideas are in your mind, read the following statement:

Bees are nothing but pests.

If you were told you had to agree with this statement, how would you feel? If you had to disagree, how would you feel? Write as many points as you can to show why people might agree and as many as you can to show why they might disagree with this statement. Begin by making a general statement about bees.

Discussion

25 — From Tommy Tadpole to Thomas Frog

Although we change as we grow, we are born with a body that increases in size but doesn't change its entire form. When a tadpole hatches from an egg it looks a little like a fish and it lives only in water, breathing through gills. Eventually, the tadpole grows lungs and legs and is able to hop around on land—it becomes a frog.

Research the life cycle of a frog and, using the information on this card as a guide, write a report about the amazing changes that take place during the life cycle of this amphibious creature.

Report

---

26 — An amazing work of art

If you've ever had a close look at a bird's nest you were probably amazed when you saw the detail that these creatures put into building a safe place in which to lay their eggs. We could spend hours trying to gather the right twigs, bits of fluff, leaves and other materials that a bird uses to build a nest but we would not be able to create a work of art equal to that of a bird.

If you were able to study a real bird's nest it would be a great advantage. If you can't, perhaps you can find a picture of one or rely on what you have observed in the past. Providing as much information as possible, explain how a bird manages to create such an amazing little construction that holds not only the weight of the mother but eggs and eventually baby birds.

Explanation

27 Cracked open

People eat the eggs of a number of different animals. Probably the most commonly eaten egg is that of a hen. Eggs are often eaten by themselves but are also used in making many other types of foods such as cakes and biscuits. Some people even eat eggs without cooking them.

To cook an egg the way you enjoy it you need to follow certain steps. You are going to write detailed instructions on how to cook an egg in your chosen way. You might choose a boiled egg, a fried egg or an omelette. You must begin by listing all the materials that you will need, such as an egg, a fork and a pan. Once you have done this write your instructions in order so that someone would be able to read them and cook an egg in your chosen way.

Procedure

28 Tiny but so strong

An ant never grows to be very big if we compare it to other creatures such as a bird, a dog or a cat. Ants begin life in little eggs and when they hatch from these they are usually white, have no legs and are called larvae. When they grow, some ants are known as workers, some are called soldiers and others are queens. All of them have different jobs to do in an ant nest. Although they are only tiny, ants can be very clever. Read and think about this statement.

An ant is the strongest of all creatures because although it is only tiny, it can carry and drag objects bigger than itself.

Decide whether or not you agree with this statement. Once you have made up your mind, write as many points as you can to support your decision.

Discussion

29 Way back then

Now that you are in the middle of primary school you probably think a little differently from the way you did when you first started school. You probably enjoy different things and, more than likely, you look a little different. You are moving through changes in your life cycle.

Think back to when you started school. Think about what you loved to do and who your friends were. Try to recall a very special event during that year—perhaps a concert for your parents, a Christmas party or a visit to an extra special place. Write about all that you remember of that special day.

Recount

---

30 An amazing experience

Can you imagine being a caterpillar for part of your life, then having wings and being able to fly during another part of it? The butterfly is a very unusual creature and goes through these dramatic changes in its relatively short life. Use a number of different resources to help you find out a little more about this creature.

It's imagination time. You are about to travel through such a life cycle. You need to pretend you are no longer a person but a butterfly or a caterpillar. Write an imaginative story about some of your experiences. Remember to include an introduction, complication and resolution.

Narrative

31 Day and night

During any 24-hour period we experience both day and night. Most people are active during the day and sleep at night. The sun provides us with light during the day and on most nights we can see the moon and stars shining above. How does this happen? There is no magic switch that makes it change from darkness to light, so what makes this amazing change occur?

Use as many different resources as possible and read about day and night. Take some brief notes while you are reading. When you think you have enough information, write a text explaining how we experience both day and night during each 24-hour period.

Explanation

---

32 Memories that will last forever

We are often able to remember things that we did for the first time; for example, our first day at school, our first visit to the dentist, or our first trip on an aeroplane. Sometimes, if we really want to remember an event, it helps to write down some important details in a journal. Years later we can read the journal and memories will come flooding back.

Yesterday you created history. You landed on Mars. Mars is very different from Earth. At the end of an amazing day you decided that you wanted to remember every detail of your experience so you wrote a recount of all that happened. What did your recount say?

Recount

33 Ready to blast off

There are many household items we can recycle. You're going to use some old cardboard cylinders to construct a rocket. Of course you will need some other materials as well. Perhaps some extra cardboard, cellophane and paint might come in handy. Draw and label a basic sketch of your rocket, showing where you will use particular materials.

Once you know how you are going to construct your rocket, you need to write detailed instructions to show the procedure you will follow. Begin by listing all the materials that will be needed, including items such as scissors and glue. Follow this with ordered instructions that could easily be followed by a friend.

Procedure

---

34 How should the money be used?

Every year throughout the world, millions of pounds are spent on space travel and exploration. By travelling into space, humanity has learned a great deal about the solar system and how Earth compares to other planets far away. But for these discoveries to be made, an enormous amount of money has to be spent. Read the following statement and decide whether or not you agree with it.

There should be less space travel and all the money that is saved should be used to help the poor countries of the world.

When you have decided how you feel about the statement, write as many points as you can to show why you think that way. Begin your text by making a general statement about the way you feel; for example, 'Too much money is spent on space travel' or 'Countries should continue to spend a great deal of money on space travel'.

Discussion

35 An unbelievable sighting

Imagine studying for years to become an astronaut and learning all about the incredible things that other space explorers have seen when they've been far away in their spaceships. How exciting it would be to be told that you were about to make your first trip up beyond Earth's atmosphere. Imagine the thoughts that would flash through your mind.

Plan and write a story about an astronaut's first journey into space. During this journey the astronaut (you) and the rest of the crew see a most incredible sight. What is it? How do you feel? What happens? Don't forget your story needs to have an introduction, a complication and a resolution.

Narrative

---

36 An amazing event in history

Over the years people have made some amazing discoveries about space. Some of these discoveries have been made by people looking through very strong telescopes and others have been made by people who have actually travelled into space. Use different resources to help you learn about one of the following:

- **the discovery of one of the planets**
- **mankind's first landing on the moon**
- **Yuri Gagarin, the first man to orbit Earth**

Take notes while you read about your chosen topic. Use these notes to help you write an historical report about that topic. It is important that all your information is factual. Begin your report by making a general statement about your topic, such as 'Pluto is one of the nine planets of the solar system'.

Report

37 The seasons

Every year on Earth we experience the seasons of summer, autumn, winter and spring. As the seasons change, so do the weather conditions. It gets warmer or colder, wetter or drier and during certain periods we will have stronger winds or heavier fogs.

Use different resources to help you collect information about the seasons and why they occur. In your own words and with the help of simple diagrams, explain how and why we experience the four seasons each year.

Explanation

---

38 Oh, what a feeling

The weather can sometimes affect the way we feel. If for some reason our bodies are feeling uncomfortable due to temperature, we may feel unhappy, exhausted, miserable or frustrated. It's not always possible to feel just the way we want to because weather conditions can change unexpectedly or we may have to travel to somewhere quite unplanned.

Try to recall an occasion on which the heat of the sun or the chill in the air made you feel quite uncomfortable. Write about your experience, telling where you were, who you were with, what you were doing, how you felt and whether or not you were able to make the situation any better for yourself.

Recount

39 Locating information

When we want to find out information we sometimes think it would be best if someone simply told us what we want to know. However, if we really want to learn and remember that information, it is better if we have to go to a little trouble to find out. It's the process of locating and then reading the information that helps it to sink into our minds and stay there.

If you were asked to find out all you could about Neil Armstrong, how would you go about it? Write out the procedure that you would go through to locate this information. Once you have written this, follow your own procedure and read as much information as you can about this man.

Procedure

---

40 Put it in writing

When anything of importance happens in the world it is usually recorded in newspapers in many different countries. People like to read about what is happening on their planet and by reading such information they form opinions about all sorts of events and occurrences.

Imagine that you work for one of the largest newspaper companies in your country. Something amazing has just happened. Scientists have announced the discovery of a new planet in our solar system and you have been sent to interview these scientists. Following your interview you have to write a report for your newspaper. Your heading for your article will have to be captivating. Inform your readers, in great detail, about this recent discovery.

Report

41

Before electricity

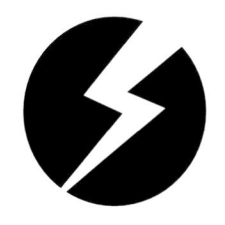

We sometimes take electricity for granted. If we want to light up a room, we flick a switch. We want to get warm, so we turn on the heater. We want to cook toast, and we get out the toaster. Many, many times each day we use electricity. However, people have not always had electricity and they were still able to do all these things.

If you had to prepare a meal without using any electricity, how would you go about it? You need to plan your meal carefully. At least one part of the meal needs to consist of a hot food. List what you will need for the preparation and then write out the steps you will follow to make the meal.

Procedure

42

The windmill

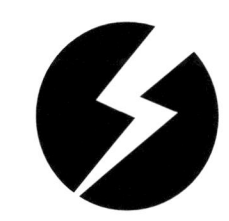

Before the invention of electricity, farmers used windmills to pump water for their crops. In fact there are some farmers who still use wind power for this purpose today. There was a lot more to a windmill than just a switch. It's time to find out how they worked.

Use the computer and books to help you find out how a windmill was made and how it operated. In your own words, explain how this machine worked. Begin by making a simple statement about a windmill and follow this with details about its different parts and how they worked. You could conclude your explanation by writing about when and where windmills were used.

Explanation

43 Through the eyes of a spider

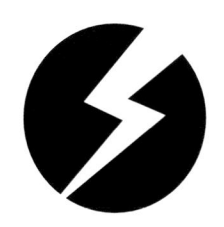

A spider can often live inside a house for quite a while before it is spotted. What a view of our home a spider would have if it spent even just one day roaming from room to room, resting now and then in a corner of the ceiling. From its vantage point high above it would be amazed at how many times in one day we human beings use electricity.

Write a story about how a spider spent a day observing how many times, and for how many different purposes, people in one house used electricity. Your story could begin with the alarm clock going off in the morning and end with the electric blanket being switched on in the evening. I wonder what it saw in between these times!

Narrative

---

44 Experimenting with magnets

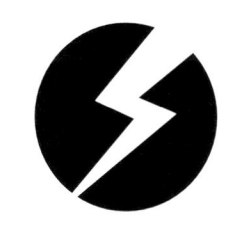

It can be a great deal of fun playing with a magnet. A magnet is a piece of metal that is able to attract certain other metallic objects. It has an end called the south pole and one called the north pole. Think for a little while about an experiment with a magnet that you would like to do. It might be about seeing what objects can be picked up by a magnet or about finding out if objects can be dragged along by a magnet.

Once you have come up with an idea for your experiment, you need to put it in written form. Begin by writing a sentence about what you are trying to discover. Once you've done that, list all the materials you will need and then write a clear procedure that will be followed during the experiment. If you are able to carry out the experiment, you can write a conclusion.

Procedure

45 When I was young

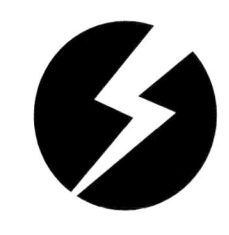

If you speak to your grandparents about when they were young they will tell you that life was quite different when they were your age. It was even more different when your great-grandparents were young. Things that we take for granted such as mobile phones, microwave ovens, even computers and televisions are only relatively recent inventions.

The following verse from a poem is the beginning of a recount about life in the past. You need to write three more verses, beginning each verse with:

When I was young, some time ago.

When I was young, some time ago
I loved to ride the trains.
The steam would pour from the chimney stacks
As we raced across the plains.

Recount

---

46 Do we use too much electricity?

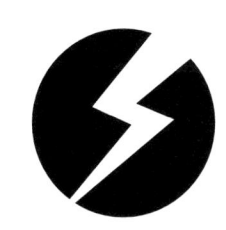

There are many purposes for which we use electricity and sometimes it is hard for us to imagine not being able to simply turn on a switch when we want something to work. How many times do we use electricity unnecessarily in one day? Are there other alternatives to using electricity or should we just make use of this source of power because it is connected to our homes?

Read and think about the following statement:

People use too much electricity.

Write a simple statement about electricity such as 'Electricity is a source of power that we use every day'. Then write points why people might agree with this statement. Once you have done this, write points why people might disagree with it.

Discussion

47 We need the sun

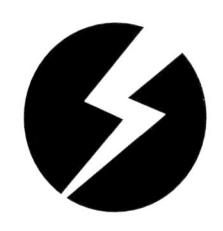

There is nothing we can do without energy. Even breathing requires energy. So too do walking and talking. But how do we get the energy to do such simple tasks? Of course we know that we need to eat to stay healthy, but how does eating give us energy? There is something extra special about the sun and the way it is able to transfer energy into our bodies.

Do some research on the sun and on energy and take notes on any information that tells you about the sun being the source of all energy. Look for points about what effect the sun has on plants and then try to think about what animals and people do to plants. When you have enough information, write an explanation about how the sun gives us energy.

Explanation

---

48 Fossil fuels

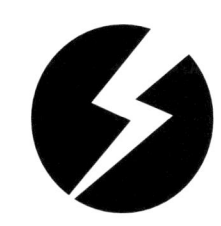

Fossil fuels, such as coal, gas and oil, are fuels that come from broken down or decomposed matter, and they will not last forever. Unlike wind energy and solar energy which are renewable, fossil fuels will one day all be used.

Find out about how fossil fuels are made and for what purpose they are used. Use your information to help you write a report about why we should be taking great care not to overuse these precious resources. In your report you include a section on how we could make better use of other sources of power.

Report

49 The ride of my life

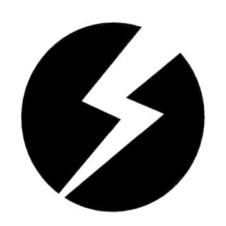

Steam trains are still used in some places today, but they are generally used more as a tourist attraction than as a means of travelling from one place to another. It is not an easy ride for those responsible for powering these vehicles, but what a fascinating job it must be.

While on holiday in a little country town, your parents become very friendly with the person who operates a scenic steam train company. On the day before you are to return home, this person asks your parents if you would be able to travel on the steam train for the day, working with the fireman who keeps the fire burning, changing water to steam. Your parents agree. Write about the day's experience.

Narrative

---

50 Safety first

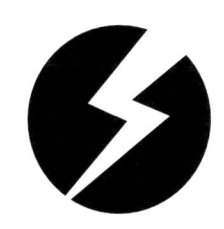

In nearly every room of your home there are probably power points, cords and appliances that show where electrical power can be used. These appliances could include heaters, kettles, radios and washing machines. Think about your home for a minute and picture all the places in which some form of power can be used. Power is extremely valuable, but at the same time it can be very dangerous if certain precautions are not taken.

Write a report telling how your home is a safety conscious home. Begin by making a statement about electrical power being used in your home and then write about all the safety measures that are taken so that no-one will be injured. These could include covers over power points, no cords left hanging down, and toddlers being kept out of the kitchen.

Report

51 — Is there time to be bored?

You've probably heard your parents say that when they were young they were able to amuse themselves and they didn't have nearly as many toys or sources of entertainment as you have today.

Do you think children have reasons to be bored in this day and age or not?

Your answer to this question is going to be a personal opinion, not that of your parents or your friends. You will need to think of children of all ages, what they have to amuse themselves, how they use their time and whether or not they could be making better use of 'free time'. Begin by making a statement about what you think and then explain why you feel that way.

Discussion

---

52 — The greatest day

Don't you just love school holidays? It doesn't really seem to matter how much we love going to school, there is nothing quite like being on holiday. Perhaps that's because we don't have to watch the clock all the time or because we are able to do more things when we choose to do them.

Recall your last school holiday. Think about all the things you did and then choose the most exciting experience of all. It might be a day you went on a day trip or visiting friends or it might be a day when you stayed home and did something exciting. Once you have made your decision, write a recount of your chosen day.

Recount

53 My favourite toy

You probably have one or two toys at home that are able to move in some way. It might be a vehicle that moves along or a figure that is able to move its limbs or a doll that is able to talk. None of these toys is able to produce its movement or sound without some form of energy being used.

Explain how your toy is able to work the way it does. You will need to write such things as, 'A key is used to wind up a spring which ….' or 'A battery is placed in a certain position and …'.

Write as much detail as you can, not simply one sentence, about the movement. Draw a labelled diagram to support your explanation.

Explanation

---

54 A new board game

You've probably played a number of different board games over the years. Board games can be a lot of fun because they can be played with friends, they can be challenging and they can also involve a great deal of luck. Some board games involve using dice, selection cards or spinning discs.

Use a large sheet of cardboard to draw up your own board game. You will need to mark clearly the spaces along which you will move, and the start and end of the game. Perhaps you will need to make selection cards or a disc that can be spun to decide moves. Once your board is constructed, write out very clear and detailed instructions on how to play the game.

Procedure

55 Inside and outside

There are many different ways in which we can use our leisure time. Some people think that leisure time should be spent sitting down doing something relaxing such as watching television, reading a book or playing a game. Others believe it should be spent swimming, jogging or riding a bike.

Read the following statement:

Children should spend part of their leisure time inside and part of their leisure time outside.

Decide how you feel about this statement. Do you agree or disagree? Once you have made up your mind, write a text explaining why you feel the way you do.

Discussion

---

56 A star for one show

There are probably a number of different television shows that you watch during a week. And you've probably wondered sometimes what it would be like to be a particular character. How are some children chosen to be actors? How do they make their characters seem so true-to-life?

Think of a show that you really enjoy watching. Picture your favourite character and then ... try to picture yourself as that character. For one show only, you have been asked to play the part of that star.

Write about what happens in that particular show. As it is a narrative, you will need to include an introduction, complication and resolution.

Narrative

57 So much time for fun

Life seems so full of leisure time when we go away for a holiday. It seems that this is a time when we can make decisions about what to do and when to do it without having to worry about too many other things. Our time seems to be more or less our own.

Imagine that you are having a wonderful holiday somewhere far away. Each day you have been doing many different things and you are keen to tell your friend at home all about your experiences. Find a piece of cardboard about the size of a large postcard. On one side draw a picture that shows where you are staying and on the other side write a letter to your friend about what you have been doing.

Recount

58 How a jack-in-the-box works

There are toys that are found in only a few countries and there are others that can be found almost everywhere in the world. The jack-in-the-box is one that can be found in many different countries and has been around for decades. Of course, there are all different types of these toys, but generally, a simple action is carried out and Jack jumps out of his box.

In your own words explain how you think a jack-in-the-box works. Begin by making a statement about what this toy is and then write about how Jack is put into action. You can conclude by drawing a labelled picture of the toy.

Explanation

59 Warnings are important

Toys and games that we use during our leisure time are often made up of a number of parts. Some of these parts can be very tiny—dice, plastic blocks, and doll's shoes for example. Not only can these parts be hard to find if we lose them, they can cause all sorts of other problems. These tiny pieces can be very dangerous to young children if used in the wrong way.

Because small parts of toys and games can be dangerous, all packets and boxes containing such pieces should carry a warning note to those who are buying these products.

Do you agree or disagree with this statement?

Write about how you feel, giving reasons and explanations.

Discussion

---

60 How do we spend our time?

Children in your class probably spend their leisure time doing a variety of activities. Some will prefer to be inside while others will spend as much spare time as possible outside.

Draw up a chart so that you can survey the children in your class about their spare time. You need to ask them whether they prefer spending their spare time inside or outside. Some will answer inside, some outside and some will probably say both. Therefore you need to have three columns ready for their answers. When you have recorded the answers from all children, check your results and see what they tell you. Write a report about the results that tells where the children in your class prefer to spend their leisure time.

Report